foreword

Some foods just taste better when washed down with a cold one. Pizza... nachos...chicken wings...mmmm. But beer can also be used in food! It adds a complexity and depth of flavour to many recipes. The yeast and carbonation also work wonders in baking, making breads light and moist. And we all know how crisp and delicious a good beer batter can be.

Cooking with beer can be a bit tricky, so remember to pair the right beer with the right dish. Wheat ales are great with chicken, fish and seafood; dark beers work well with heartier pork, beef and lamb dishes; and fruity beers can be used in desserts. Beer also becomes more bitter the longer it cooks, so don't add it too soon. And never cook with a beer you wouldn't drink—if it's not worth drinking, it's not worth adding to a recipe.

Now grab your brewski, flip through these recipes and get ready to create some culinary magic cooking with beer! (And don't forget, "one for the pot, one for the cook.")

Jean Paré

shrimp in beer batter

Perfectly cooked in a crisp, light batter, these succulent shrimp will make your mouth water.

All-purpose flour	1 cup	250 mL
Salt	1 tsp.	5 mL
Beer	1 cup	250 mL
Cooking oil	2 tbsp.	30 mL
Egg white (large)	1	1
Raw large shrimp (tails intact), peeled and deveined	1 lb.	454 g
Cooking oil, for deep-frying		
HONEY MUSTARD DIPPING SAUCE		
Grainy mustard	1/4 cup	60 mL
Liquid honey	3 tbsp.	45 mL

Combine first 4 ingredients in large bowl. Cover. Let stand for 1 hour.

Beat egg white in small bowl until soft peaks form. Fold into batter.

Holding shrimp by tail, dip into batter. Deep-fry, in 2 to 3 batches, in hot (375°F, 190°C) cooking oil for about 3 minutes until golden. Makes about 23 shrimp.

Honey Mustard Dipping Sauce: Combine mustard and honey in separate small bowl. Serve with shrimp.

1 shrimp with about 3/4 tsp. (4 mL) sauce: 96 Calories; 4.3 g Total Fat (2.2 g Mono, 1.4 g Poly, 0.4 g Sat); 33 mg Cholesterol; 8 g Carbohydrate; trace Fibre; 5 g Protein; 189 mg Sodium

tempura

*Keys to tasty, crispy tempura are a very light mixing of the batter—lumps
are GOOD—and using an ice cold liquid, preferably one that is carbonated.
To avoid greasy, soggy tempura, it is important to maintain the proper
temperature of the oil.*

Peanut oil, for deep frying

Large egg, beaten	1	1
Cold beer	1 cup	250 mL
Dry white wine	2 tbsp.	30 mL
All-purpose flour	1/2 cup	125 mL
Rice flour	1/4 cup	60 mL
Cornstarch	1/4 cup	60 mL
Zucchini slices	1/2 cup	125 mL
Broccoli florets	1/2 cup	125 mL
Sweet potato slices	1/2 cup	125 mL
Shrimp, medium, peeled and deveined	1 cup	250 mL

Heat peanut oil in pan or deep fryer until temperature is 375°F (190°C).

Combine egg, beer and white wine in small bowl.

In another bowl, combine flour, rice flour and cornstarch. Add liquid to dry
mixture and very lightly mix together. The batter should look lumpy. Dip
vegetables and seafood in tempura batter and fry in small batches until
golden and crispy. Serves 6.

1 serving: *130 Calories; 3.5 g Total Fat (1.5 g Mono, 0.5 g Poly, 0.5 g Sat);
30 mg Cholesterol; 18 g Carbohydrate; <1 g Fibre; 4 g Protein; 25 mg Sodium*

onion fritters

Experiment with the type of onion you use for these tasty fritters—Vidalia or Walla Walla onions will lend a little sweetness, or for a touch of heat go with a Spanish onion.

Beer	3/4 cup	175 mL
All-purpose flour	3/4 cup	175 mL
Sugar	1/2 tsp.	2 mL
Salt	1/4 tsp.	1 mL
Pepper	1/8 tsp.	0.5 mL
Chopped onion	3/4 cup	175 mL

Mix first 5 ingredients together. Let stand for at least 2 hours.

Stir in onion. Drop by the spoonful into hot (375ºF, 190ºC) cooking oil and cook until light brown. Serves 6.

1 serving: 160 Calories; 9 g Total Fat (6 g Mono, 2.5 g Poly, 0.5 g Sat); 0 mg Cholesterol; 15 g Carbohydrate; <1 g Fibre; 2 g Protein; 20 mg Sodium

creamy cheese dip

The addition of beer gives this cheesy dip a unique, zippy flavour. Serve with fresh vegetables and assorted crackers.

Block of cream cheese, room temperature (8 oz., 250 g)	1	1
Grated medium Cheddar cheese	2/3 cup	150 mL
Worcestershire sauce	2 tsp.	10 mL
Chopped green onion	2 tbsp.	30 mL
Beer (or alcohol-free beer)	1/4 cup	60 mL

Thinly sliced green onion, for garnish

Process first 5 ingredients in food processor until smooth. Or place in medium bowl and mash with fork until smooth. Transfer to small bowl. Cover. Chill for 2 to 3 hours to blend flavours. Let stand at room temperature for 30 minutes before serving.

Garnish with green onion. Makes 1 2/3 cups (400 mL).

2 tbsp. (30 mL): 89 Calories; 8.2 g Total Fat (2.3 g Mono, 0.3 g Poly, 5.2 g Sat); 26 mg Cholesterol; 1 g Carbohydrate; trace Fibre; 3 g Protein; 98 mg Sodium

jalapeño cheese fondue

Serve this cheesy, spicy fondue with toasted whole-grain bread cubes, bell pepper pieces or tortilla chips, and be sure to keep it warm in a dip warmer or fondue pot.

Grated jalapeño Monterey Jack cheese	2 cups	500 mL
Grated sharp Cheddar cheese	2 cups	500 mL
All-purpose flour	3 tbsp.	45 mL
Chili powder	1 tsp.	5 mL
Dry mustard	1/4 tsp.	1 mL
Garlic powder	1/4 tsp.	1 mL
Beer	1 cup	250 mL
Finely chopped fresh jalapeño pepper (see Tip, page 64)	2 tsp.	30 mL

Toss first 6 ingredients in large bowl until coated.

Combine beer and jalapeño pepper in medium saucepan on medium. Cook for about 2 minutes until hot, but not boiling. Add cheese mixture, 1 cup (250 mL) at a time, whisking after each addition until melted and smooth. Carefully pour into fondue pot. Keep warm over low flame. Makes about 2 1/2 cups (625 mL).

1/2 cup (125 mL): 379 Calories; 29.4 g Total Fat (4.3 g Mono, 0.4 g Poly, 17.5 g Sat); 87 mg Cholesterol; 7 g Carbohydrate; trace Fibre; 22 g Protein; 597 mg Sodium

holiday gingerbread bundt

This beautifully dark Bundt cake is dusted with "snow" and looks amazing topped with fresh berries. Special ingredients like cocoa, applesauce and beer contribute to the deep flavours.

Stout (or dark) beer	1 cup	250 mL
Fancy (mild) molasses	2/3 cup	150 mL
Large eggs	3	3
Brown sugar, packed	1 cup	250 mL
Unsweetened applesauce	2/3 cup	150 mL
Cooking oil	1/2 cup	125 mL
All-purpose flour	2 1/2 cups	625 mL
Cocoa, sifted if lumpy	1/4 cup	60 mL
Ground ginger	2 tbsp.	30 mL
Baking powder	1 1/2 tsp.	7 mL
Baking soda	1 tsp.	5 mL
Ground cinnamon	1 tsp.	5 mL
Ground allspice	1/2 tsp.	2 mL
Ground nutmeg	1/2 tsp.	2 mL
Salt	1/2 tsp.	2 mL
Icing (confectioner's) sugar	1 tbsp.	15 mL

Combine beer and molasses in medium saucepan. Bring to a boil on medium. Carefully transfer to medium bowl. Let stand for about 1 hour, stirring occasionally, until cooled to room temperature.

Add next 4 ingredients. Beat until brown sugar is dissolved.

Combine next 9 ingredients in large bowl. Make a well in centre. Add beer mixture to well. Beat until smooth. Spread evenly in greased 12 cup (3 L) Bundt pan. Bake in 350°F (175°C) oven for about 45 minutes until wooden pick inserted in centre comes out clean. Let stand in pan on wire rack for 10 minutes. Invert onto wire rack to cool completely.

Dust with icing sugar. Cuts into 16 pieces.

1 piece: 242 Calories; 8.3 g Total Fat (4.6 g Mono, 2.3 g Poly, 0.9 g Sat); 40 mg Cholesterol; 40 g Carbohydrate; 1 g Fibre; 3 g Protein; 225 mg Sodium

sweet rye bread loaves

Golden brown bread that is crusty on the outside but soft and moist on the inside. Perfect for dunking in a fondue.

Warm water	1/4 cup	60 mL
Granulated sugar	1 tsp.	5 mL
Active dry yeast	2 1/2 tsp.	12 mL
(or 1/4 oz., 8 g, envelope)		
Beer	1 cup	250 mL
Fancy (mild) molasses	2 tbsp.	30 mL
Butter (or hard margarine)	2 tbsp.	30 mL
Salt	1/2 tsp.	2 mL
Rye flour	1 1/2 cups	375 mL
Flaxseed (or caraway seed)	4 tsp.	20 mL
All-purpose flour	2 cups	500 mL

Stir warm water and sugar in small bowl until sugar is dissolved. Sprinkle yeast over top. Let stand for 10 minutes. Stir until yeast is dissolved.

Heat and stir next 4 ingredients in small saucepan until butter is melted. Pour into large bowl. Stir until lukewarm. Add yeast mixture. Gradually stir in rye flour and flaxseed until smooth.

Add 2/3 cup (150 mL) all-purpose flour. Stir vigorously for 2 minutes. Slowly work in remaining flour until dough pulls away from side of bowl and is no longer sticky. Turn out onto lightly floured surface. Knead for about 10 minutes until smooth and elastic. Place dough in greased bowl, turning once to grease top. Cover with greased waxed paper and tea towel. Let stand in oven with light on and door closed for about 1 1/2 hours until doubled in bulk. Punch dough down. Shape into 2 loaves. Arrange on large greased baking sheet, leaving space between to allow for rising. Cut 3 or 4 diagonal slashes across top of each loaf. Cover with tea towel. Let stand in oven with light on and door closed for about 1 hour until doubled in size. Brush loaves with water. Bake in 400°F (200°C) oven for 10 minutes. Reduce heat to 350°F (175°C). Bake for 20 to 25 minutes until golden brown and hollow-sounding when tapped. Remove to wire rack to cool. Makes 2 loaves that cut into 8 slices each.

1 slice: 129 Calories; 2.1 g Total Fat (1 g Mono, 0.5 g Poly, 0.4 g Sat); 0 mg Cholesterol; 24 g Carbohydrate; 2 g Fibre; 3 g Protein; 94 mg Sodium

sesame beer bread

A hearty bread coated in sesame seeds, with a subtle beer flavour. Good alongside soup. Because there's no fat, the bread should be eaten the same day it is baked.

All-purpose flour	3 1/4 cups	800 mL
Baking powder	1 tbsp.	15 mL
Granulated sugar	1 tbsp.	15 mL
Salt	2 tsp.	10 mL
Baking soda	1/2 tsp.	2 mL
Can of light beer (12 1/2 oz., 355 mL)	1	1
Milk	1 1/4 tsp.	6 mL
Sesame seeds	1 tbsp.	15 mL

Combine first 5 ingredients in large bowl. Make a well in centre.

Add beer to well. Stir until soft, sticky dough forms. Turn out onto lightly floured surface. Gently shape to fit greased 9 x 5 x 3 inch (23 x 12.5 x 7.5 cm) loaf pan. Place dough in pan. Press into corners if necessary.

Brush top of loaf with milk. Sprinkle with sesame seeds. Bake in 375°F (190°C) oven for about 40 minutes until golden brown and hollow-sounding when tapped. Cuts into 16 slices.

1 slice: *111 Calories; 0.6 g Total Fat (0.1 g Mono, 0.2 g Poly, 0.1 g Sat); 0 mg Cholesterol; 22 g Carbohydrate; 1 g Fibre; 3 g Protein; 408 mg Sodium*

bbq beer bread

A fabulous, golden loaf with a hint of cinnamon and beer. Spread with a bit of butter when warm and enjoy!

All-purpose flour	3 cups	750 mL
Granulated sugar	2 tbsp.	30 mL
Baking powder	4 tsp.	20 mL
Salt	1 tsp.	5 mL
Ground cinnamon	1/4 tsp.	1 mL
Can of beer (12 1/2 oz., 355 mL), room temperature	1	1
Cooking oil	1 tbsp.	15 mL
Hard margarine (or butter), softened	1 tsp.	5 mL

Measure first 5 ingredients into large bowl. Stir. Make a well in centre.

Pour beer and cooking oil into well. Mix until soft ball forms. Turn into greased 9 x 5 x 3 inch (23 x 12.5 x 7.5 cm) loaf pan. Push to fill corners. Preheat gas barbecue to medium. Turn off centre or left burner. Place pan on unlit side of grill. Close lid. Cook for about 55 minutes until risen and golden.

Brush with margarine. Turn out onto wire rack to cool. Cuts into 16 slices.

1 slice: 117 Calories; 1.4 g Total Fat (0.7 g Mono, 0.4 g Poly, 0.2 g Sat); 0 mg Cholesterol; 22 g Carbohydrate; 1 g Fibre; 3 g Protein; 245 mg Sodium

blue cheese beer burgers

Perfect for a pre-game party or a post-game get-together. The Stilton adds a pleasing, creamy sharpness. Garnish with tomato slices and pickled or roasted beets.

Finely chopped onion	1 cup	250 mL
Fine dry bread crumbs	1/2 cup	125 mL
Stout beer	1/3 cup	75 mL
Celery salt	1 tsp.	5 mL
Garlic powder	1 tsp.	5 mL
Pepper	1/2 tsp.	2 mL
Lean ground beef	2 lbs.	900 g
Stilton cheese, sliced	6 oz.	170 g
Onion buns, split	8	8

Combine first 7 ingredients in large bowl. Divide into 8 portions. Shape portions into patties, about 4 inches (10 cm) in diameter. Chill, covered, for 1 hour. Grill patties on direct medium heat for about 5 minutes per side until internal temperature reaches 160°F (71°C).

Top with cheese during final minute of cooking. Serve patties in buns. Makes 8 burgers.

1 burger: *501 Calories; 24.5 g Total Fat (7.1 g Mono, 0.5 g Poly, 11.1 g Sat);*
87 mg Cholesterol; 33 g Carbohydrate; 1 g Fibre; 34 g Protein; 795 mg Sodium

drunken lamb burgers with cranberry dijon mustard

Lamb is marinated in a bath of beer, creating a moist, hearty pattie. Top with the intriguing cranberry mustard and a garnish of lettuce and slices of red onion.

Fine dry bread crumbs	1/4 cup	60 mL
Finely chopped onion	1/4 cup	60 mL
Tomato paste (see Tip, page 64)	2 tbsp.	30 mL
Chopped fresh rosemary	2 tsp.	10 mL
Garlic cloves, minced	2	2
Salt	1/2 tsp.	2 mL
Ground allspice	1/4 tsp.	1 mL
Lean ground lamb	1 lb.	454 g
Dark or amber ale	1 cup	250 mL
Jellied cranberry sauce	1/2 cup	125 mL
Dijon mustard (with whole seeds)	1/4 cup	60 mL
Brown sugar, packed	2 tbsp.	30 mL
Buns, split	4	4

Combine first 8 ingredients and divide into 4 portions. Shape portions into patties, about 4 inches (10 cm) in diameter. Place patties in a shallow baking dish and add ale. Chill, covered, for at least 6 hours or overnight. Drain and discard marinade. Grill patties on direct medium heat for about 7 minutes per side until internal temperature reaches 160°F (71°C).

Whisk next 3 ingredients together until smooth.

Serve patties, on top of about 1 tbsp. (15 mL) cranberry mustard mixture, in buns. The remaining mustard mixture can be stored in the refrigerator for up to 1 week. Makes 4 burgers.

1 burger: 540 Calories; 29.3 g Total Fat (11.6 g Mono, 3.1 g Poly, 12.1 g Sat); 83 mg Cholesterol; 40 g Carbohydrate; 2 g Fibre; 25 g Protein; 742 mg Sodium

beer brats with apple sauerkraut

An ode to Bavaria! These tasty apple and sauerkraut brats will have you reaching for your lederhosen.

Uncooked bratwurst sausages	6	6
Sauerkraut, rinsed and drained	2 cups	500 mL
Thinly sliced onion	1 1/3 cups	325 mL
Thinly sliced tart apple (such as Granny Smith)	1 1/4 cups	300 mL
Warm beer	1 cup	250 mL
Dijon mustard	2 tbsp.	30 mL
Hot dog buns, split	6	6

Arrange sausages in single layer in 9 x 9 inch (23 x 23 cm) baking pan. Scatter next 3 ingredients over top.

Combine beer and mustard in medium bowl. Drizzle over sausage mixture. Preheat gas barbecue to medium. Place pan on ungreased grill. Close lid. Cook for 30 minutes, turning sausages occasionally. Transfer sausages from pan to greased grill. Close lid. Cook sausages, leaving pan on grill, for about 7 minutes per side until browned.

Serve sausages, topped with sauerkraut mixture, in buns. Serves 6.

1 serving: 347 Calories; 15.7 g Total Fat (6.5 g Mono, 2.5 g Poly, 5.3 g Sat); 29 mg Cholesterol; 33 g Carbohydrate; 4 g Fibre; 14 g Protein; 1364 mg Sodium

welsh rarebit

This toasted cheese sandwich makes an unusual and tasty appetizer or lunch dish.

Grated sharp Cheddar cheese	2 cups	500 mL
All-purpose flour	1 tbsp.	15 mL
Beer	1/3 cup	75 mL
Dry mustard	1 1/2 tsp.	7 mL
Fresh bread slices, toasted	4	4

Toss cheese with flour in heavy medium saucepan. Add beer and mustard. Heat on very low, stirring often, until cheese is melted and smooth. (Mixture can be prepared to this point and reheated later.)

Place toasted bread slices on small greased baking sheet. Spoon cheese mixture over toast, completely covering surface. Broil 4 inches (10 cm) from heat until bubbly and lightly browned. Broiling for too long will make cheese tough. Makes 4 rarebits.

1 rarebit: 320 Calories; 20 g Total Fat (5 g Mono, 0.5 g Poly, 12 g Sat); 60 mg Cholesterol; 21 g Carbohydrate; 3 g Fibre; 19 g Protein; 520 mg Sodium

cream ale and cheddar soup

Rich and creamy, this soup is the perfect comfort food for a cold winter's day. It is also a snap to make if you have an immersion blender.

Medium onions, diced	2	2
Olive oil	1 tbsp.	15 mL
Unsalted butter	1/4 cup	60 mL
Diced celery	2 cups	500 mL
Diced parsnips	1 cup	250 mL
Medium potatoes, peeled and diced	4	4
Bay leaf	1	1
Heavy cream (32%)	2 cups	500 mL
Sharp white Cheddar cheese, grated	2 cups	500 mL
Bottle of cream ale (12 oz, 341 mL)	1	1
Sea salt, sprinkle		
Freshly ground pepper, sprinkle		

In heavy pot, sauté onions in butter and oil until they turn golden.

Add celery, parsnips, potatoes, bay leaf and enough water or prepared vegetable or chicken broth to cover vegetables. Simmer for 15 minutes.

Add cream. Simmer for 10 to 15 minutes, until potatoes are cooked and soup is reduced and creamy.

Remove soup from heat and blend in cheese in small batches, following manufacturer's instructions for processing hot liquids.

Return to medium-low heat and stir in ale to taste. Season with salt and pepper. Serves 4.

1 serving: 830 Calories; 56 g Total Fat (17 g Mono, 2.5 g Poly, 34 g Sat); 170 mg Cholesterol; 58 g Carbohydrate; 7 g Fibre; 22 g Protein; 520 mg Sodium

barley and lamb soup

There's plenty of garden goodness in this rich lamb and barley soup, with a double dose of flavour from beer and pearl barley! This tasty soup can be stored in an airtight container in the freezer for up to three months.

Cooking oil	2 tsp.	10 mL
Lean ground lamb	1/2 lb.	225 g
Chopped onion	1 cup	250 mL
Sliced leek (white part only)	1 cup	250 mL
Diced celery	1/2 cup	125 mL
Dark beer (such as honey brown)	1 1/2 cups	375 mL
Prepared beef broth	6 cups	1.5 L
Water	2 cups	500 mL
Diced carrot	1 cup	250 mL
Diced parsnip	1 cup	250 mL
Diced yellow turnip (rutabaga)	1 cup	250 mL
Pearl barley	1/2 cup	125 mL
Tomato paste (see Tip, page 64)	1 tbsp.	15 mL
Dried rosemary, crushed	1/2 tsp.	2 mL
Dried thyme	1/2 tsp.	2 mL
Salt	3/4 tsp.	4 mL
Pepper	1/2 tsp.	2 mL
Bay leaf	1	1
Diced zucchini (with peel)	1 cup	250 mL

Heat cooking oil in Dutch oven on medium-high. Add next 4 ingredients. Scramble-fry for about 5 minutes until lamb is no longer pink.

Add beer. Heat and stir, scraping any brown bits from bottom of pan, until boiling.

Add next 12 ingredients. Stir. Bring to a boil. Reduce heat to medium-low. Simmer, covered, for about 45 minutes until barley is tender.

Add zucchini. Stir. Simmer, covered, for about 10 minutes until zucchini is tender. Skim and discard fat. Remove and discard bay leaf. Makes about 12 1/2 cups (3.1 L).

1 cup (250 mL): *113 Calories; 3.5 g Total Fat (1.5 g Mono, 0.4 g Poly, 1.1 g Sat); 12 mg Cholesterol; 14 g Carbohydrate; 3 g Fibre; 5 g Protein; 730 mg Sodium*

mushroom barsotto

Everyone knows about rice risotto, but barley can also be used to make this rich and creamy dish. Hearty flavours make this a great side for roast beef or pork. For best results, make the beer a honey brown or amber ale.

Olive oil	1 tbsp.	15 mL
Chopped portobello mushrooms (about 12 oz., 340 g)	5 cups	1.25 L
Prepared vegetable broth	4 cups	1 L
Water	2 cups	500 mL
Olive oil	1 tbsp.	15 mL
Chopped onion	1 cup	250 mL
Pearl barley	1 cup	250 mL
Dark (or alcohol-free) beer	3/4 cup	175 mL
Grated Asiago cheese	1/3 cup	75 mL
Pepper	1/2 tsp.	2 mL

Heat first amount of olive oil in large frying pan on medium-high. Add mushrooms. Cook for 5 to 10 minutes, stirring occasionally, until mushrooms are starting to brown and liquid is evaporated. Remove from heat. Set aside.

Combine broth and water in medium saucepan. Bring to a boil. Reduce heat to low. Cover to keep hot.

Heat second amount of olive oil in large saucepan on medium. Add onion. Cook for about 10 minutes, stirring occasionally, until starting to soften.

Add barley. Heat and stir until coated. Add beer. Heat and stir until liquid is absorbed. Add 1 ladle-full (about 1/2 cup, 125 mL) broth mixture. Heat and stir until almost absorbed. Repeat with remaining broth mixture, adding 1 ladle at a time, until broth mixture is absorbed and barley is tender. Add mushrooms. Cook and stir until heated through.

Add cheese and pepper. Stir. Makes about 5 cups (1.25 L).

1 cup (250 mL): 276 Calories; 8.3 g Total Fat (4.0 g Mono, 0.7 g Poly, 2.1 g Sat); 6 mg Cholesterol; 42 g Carbohydrate; 8 g Fibre; 8 g Protein; 830 mg Sodium

seared beef carpaccio

Peppery, thinly sliced beef and mushrooms sautéed in beer and green peppercorns unite with the natural zing of arugula. For best results, choose a pale ale or pale lager.

Montreal steak spice	1 tbsp.	15 mL
Chopped fresh thyme	1 tbsp.	15 mL
Beef strip loin steak	1 lb.	454 g
Cooking oil	1 tbsp.	15 mL
Sliced brown mushrooms	5 cups	1.25 L
Beer	1/3 cup	75 mL
Canned green peppercorns	1 tbsp.	15 mL
Butter	1 tbsp.	15 mL
Arugula leaves, lightly packed	1/2 cup	125 mL

Combine steak spice and thyme. Press steak into spice mixture until coated. Cook on greased grill on high for about 2 minutes per side until browned and slightly crisp. Transfer to cutting board. Cover with foil and let stand for 10 minutes.

Heat cooking oil in large frying pan on medium-high. Add mushrooms and cook until browned and liquid has evaporated.

Stir in beer and peppercorns. Add butter and stir until melted.

Cut steak across the grain into very thin slices. Arrange with arugula and mushrooms on serving plate. Serves 6.

1 serving: 250 Calories; 15.7 g Total Fat (6.7 g Mono, 1.2 g Poly, 6.0 g Sat); 47 mg Cholesterol; 3 g Carbohydrate; 1 g Fibre; 17 g Protein; 391 mg Sodium

beef carbonnade

This easy-to-make stew, originating in Belgium, typically contains bacon, beer and lots of onions.

Bacon slices	4	4
Inside round steak, (or boneless chuck) trimmed of fat and cut into 1 inch (2.5 cm) cubes	1 1/2 lbs.	680 g
Pepper, sprinkle		
Medium onions, cut lengthwise and sliced	3	3
Garlic clove, minced	1	1
Brown sugar, packed	1 tbsp.	15 mL
Beer (12 1/2 oz., 355 mL)	1	1
Can of condensed beef broth (10 oz., 284 mL)	1	1
Bay leaf	1	1
Red wine vinegar	1 tbsp.	15 mL
Cornstarch	1 tbsp.	15 mL
Chopped fresh parsley	1 tbsp.	15 mL

Cook bacon in large pot until crisp. Remove to paper towel with slotted spoon, reserving 2 tsp. (10 mL) drippings in pot. Crumble. Set aside.

Cook beef in reserved bacon drippings in same pot on medium-high. Sprinkle with pepper. When browned on all sides, transfer to medium bowl, reserving any drippings in pot.

Add onion to pot. Cook on medium, stirring occasionally, until soft. Add garlic and brown sugar. Cook on medium-low until onion is browned and very soft. Stir in beer, broth and bay leaf. Bring to a boil. Add beef. Stir. Reduce heat. Cover. Simmer for about 1 1/2 hours, stirring occasionally, until beef is very tender. Remove and discard bay leaf.

Stir wine vinegar into cornstarch in small cup. Stir into beef mixture. Heat and stir until boiling and slightly thickened.

Sprinkle individual servings with reserved bacon and parsley. Serves 6.

1 serving: 240 Calories; 6.2 g Total Fat (2.7 g Mono, 0.6 g Poly, 2.3 g Sat); 54 mg Cholesterol; 11 g Carbohydrate; 1 g Fibre; 29 g Protein; 450 mg Sodium

beer and bacon chicken

Delightfully tender chicken in a smoky bacon and beer sauce. Delicious served with buttered carrots and mashed potatoes.

All-purpose flour	3 tbsp.	45 mL
Chicken drumsticks, skin removed	12	12
Bacon slices, cooked crisp and crumbled	4	4
Can of beer (12 1/2 oz., 355 mL)	1	1
Prepared chicken broth	1/2 cup	125 mL
Worcestershire sauce	1 tbsp.	15 mL
Chopped fresh oregano leaves (or 3/4 tsp., 4 mL, dried)	1 tbsp.	15 mL
Chopped fresh thyme leaves (or 1/2 tsp., 2 mL, dried)	2 tsp.	10 mL
Salt	1/4 tsp.	1 mL
Pepper	1/4 tsp.	1 mL
Water	1 tbsp.	15 mL
Cornstarch	2 tsp.	10 mL

Measure flour into large resealable freezer bag. Add 1/2 of chicken. Seal bag. Toss until coated. Repeat with remaining chicken. Put chicken into 3 1/2 to 4 quart (3.5 to 4 L) slow cooker.

Combine next 8 ingredients in 4 cup (1 L) liquid measure. Pour over chicken. Stir. Cover. Cook on Low for 8 to 9 hours or on High for 4 to 4 1/2 hours. Carefully remove chicken with slotted spoon to large serving bowl. Cover to keep warm.

Stir water into cornstarch in small cup until smooth. Add to liquid in slow cooker. Stir well. Cover. Cook on High for about 15 minutes until thickened. Pour over chicken. Serves 6.

1 serving: 234 Calories; 8.9 g Total Fat (3.1 g Mono, 1.9 g Poly, 2.5 g Sat); 98 mg Cholesterol; 7 g Carbohydrate; trace Fibre; 26 g Protein; 268 mg Sodium

beer can chicken

Check the barbecue section of your local department store for a roasting stand that is specially made to hold the beer can and chicken safely.

Can of beer (12 1/2 oz., 355 mL)	1	1
Apple juice	1/4 cup	60 mL
Apple cider vinegar	2 tbsp.	30 mL
Cooking oil	2 tbsp.	30 mL
Worcestershire sauce	2 tsp.	10 mL
Montreal chicken spice	2 tbsp.	30 mL
Brown sugar, packed	2 tsp.	10 mL
Dried oregano	1 tsp.	5 mL
Dry mustard	1 tsp.	5 mL
Onion powder	1 tsp.	5 mL
Whole chicken	4 lbs.	1.8 kg

Pour 2/3 cup (150 mL) beer into a spray bottle, leaving remaining beer in can. Set can aside. Add next 4 ingredients to spray bottle. Swirl gently to combine. Set aside.

Combine next 5 ingredients in small bowl. Sprinkle 1 tbsp. (15 mL) seasoning mixture inside chicken cavity. Rub remaining seasoning mixture over surface of chicken. Let stand, covered, in refrigerator for 30 minutes. Stand chicken, tail end down, over beer can and press down to insert can into body cavity. Preheat gas barbecue to medium. Place drip pan under grill on one side of barbecue. Balance chicken upright over drip pan, so that bottom of beer can rests on grill. Turn burner under chicken to low, leaving opposite burner on medium. Close lid. Cook for 1 1/2 to 1 3/4 hours, spraying chicken with beer mixture every 20 minutes, until browned and meat thermometer inserted in thickest part of breast reads 180°F (83°C). Remove chicken from beer can by inserting a carving fork through chicken above level of top of beer can and lifting chicken off of can, taking care not to spill the contents of can, as liquid will be extremely hot. Transfer chicken to cutting board. Cover with foil. Let stand for 10 minutes before carving. Serves 6.

1 serving: 754 Calories; 50.4 g Total Fat (21.6 g Mono, 11.1 g Poly, 13.4 g Sat); 227 mg Cholesterol; 10 g Carbohydrate; trace Fibre; 57 g Protein; 607 mg Sodium

sausage and beer risotto

We have suggested using hot sausages for this thick, creamy risotto, but you can use any kind you like.

Olive (or cooking) oil	2 tsp.	10 mL
Hot Italian sausages, casings removed (about 6)	1 1/4 lbs.	560 g
Prepared chicken broth	7 1/2 cups	1.9 L
Olive (or cooking) oil	1 tbsp.	15 mL
Finely chopped onion	1 1/2 cups	375 mL
Garlic cloves, minced	4	4
Arborio rice	2 1/2 cups	625 mL
Beer	3/4 cup	175 mL
Chopped fresh parsley	1/3 cup	75 mL
Salt, sprinkle		
Pepper, sprinkle		
Finely grated fresh Parmesan cheese	2/3 cup	150 mL

Heat first amount of olive oil in large frying pan on medium. Cook sausages for about 15 minutes, turning occasionally, until plump. Remove from pan. Cut into 1/2 inch (12 mm) pieces. Set aside.

Pour broth into large saucepan. Cover. Bring to a boil. Reduce heat to low. Keep warm.

Heat second amount of olive oil in large pot or Dutch oven on medium-low. Add onion and garlic. Cook for about 10 minutes, stirring occasionally, until onion is soft.

Add rice. Stir until rice is coated with olive oil. Add beer. Heat and stir on medium until beer is absorbed. Add hot broth, 1 cup (250 mL) at a time, stirring until broth is absorbed before adding more. Repeat with remaining broth, stirring constantly, until all broth is absorbed and rice is tender, about 25 to 30 minutes.

Add sausage and next 3 ingredients. Stir until sausage is hot. Remove from heat. Stir in Parmesan cheese. Makes about 8 cups (2 L). Serves 6.

1 serving: 811 Calories; 39 g Total Fat (18.2 g Mono, 4.7 g Poly, 13.9 g Sat); 80 mg Cholesterol; 78 g Carbohydrate; 1 g Fibre; 31 g Protein; 1932 mg Sodium

pork, beer and fruit stew

Serve this rich, flavourful stew over rice or couscous.

All-purpose flour	1/4 cup	60 mL
Salt, sprinkle		
Boneless pork shoulder blade steak, trimmed of fat, cut into 3/4 inch (2 cm) pieces	2 lbs.	900 g
Cooking oil	4 tsp.	20 mL
Cooking oil	2 tsp.	10 mL
Chopped onion	1 1/2 cups	375 mL
Garlic cloves, minced	2	2
Ground coriander	1/2 tsp.	2 mL
Ground cumin	1/4 tsp.	1 mL
Salt	1/4 tsp.	1 mL
Prepared chicken broth	1 cup	250 mL
Dark beer (such as honey brown)	1 cup	250 mL
Apple juice	1/2 cup	125 mL
Dijon mustard	1 tbsp.	15 mL
Dried apricots, halved	1 cup	250 mL
Pitted prunes, halved	1/2 cup	125 mL

Combine flour and salt in large resealable freezer bag. Add half of pork. Toss until coated. Transfer pork to plate. Repeat with remaining pork. Reserve any remaining flour mixture. Heat half of first amount of cooking oil in large frying pan on medium. Cook pork, in 2 batches, for about 5 minutes, stirring occasionally, adding more cooking oil if necessary, until browned. Transfer to 3 1/2 to 4 quart (3.5 to 4 L) slow cooker.

Heat second amount of cooking oil in same frying pan. Add onion. Cook for about 5 minutes, stirring often, until starting to soften.

Add next 4 ingredients and reserved flour mixture. Heat and stir for 1 minute. Slowly add broth, stirring constantly until smooth. Add next 3 ingredients. Heat and stir, scraping any brown bits from bottom of pan, until boiling and thickened. Pour over pork. Stir. Scatter apricots and prunes over top. Cook, covered, on Low for 8 to 10 hours or on High for 4 to 5 hours. Stir. Makes about 6 cups (1.5 L).

1 cup (250 mL): 428 Calories; 14.3 g Total Fat (7.1 g Mono, 2.5 g Poly, 3.6 g Sat); 98 mg Cholesterol; 37 g Carbohydrate; 3 g Fibre; 33 g Protein; 394 mg Sodium

barbecue beer ribs

These sweet, smoky ribs are coated in a crunchy, dark glaze. The addition of beer creates a unique and appealing flavour.

Pork back ribs, cut into 3-bone portions	4 lbs.	1.8 kg
Dry sherry	1 cup	250 mL
Can of beer (12 1/2 oz., 355 mL)	1	1
Brown sugar, packed	2/3 cup	150 mL
Soy sauce	1/2 cup	125 mL
Barbecue sauce	1/2 cup	125 mL
Liquid honey	1/4 cup	60 mL
Garlic cloves, minced (or 3/4 tsp., 4 mL, powder)	3	3

Combine ribs and sherry in large pot or Dutch oven. Add water to cover. Bring to a boil. Reduce heat to medium-low. Simmer, uncovered, for about 1 1/2 hours, skimming off fat occasionally, until ribs are tender. Remove ribs to wire rack over baking sheet with sides to drain and cool. Discard liquid and solids in pot. Place ribs in large resealable freezer bag.

For the marinade, combine all 6 ingredients in medium saucepan. Heat and stir on medium until boiling and brown sugar is dissolved. Cool. Pour over ribs. Seal. Turn until coated. Marinate in refrigerator for at least 3 hours, turning several times. Remove ribs, reserving 1/2 cup (125 mL) marinade. Boil marinade in small saucepan for 5 minutes. Preheat gas barbecue to medium-high. Place ribs on greased grill. Close lid. Cook for about 5 minutes per side, brushing with reserved marinade, until heated through. Serves 6.

1 serving: 674 Calories; 23 g Total Fat (10.4 g Mono, 2.5 g Poly, 7.9 g Sat); 143 mg Cholesterol; 43 g Carbohydrate; 1 g Fibre; 67 g Protein; 1490 mg Sodium

buffalo beer ribs

*Take ribs, a classic chicken wing sauce and a couple of cans of beer and
you get a tender show-stopper with a spicy bite!*

Pork side ribs, trimmed of fat and cut into 3-bone portions	4 lbs.	1.8 kg
Cans of beer (12 1/2 oz., 355 mL, each)	2	2
Butter (or hard margarine)	1/4 cup	60 mL
Garlic cloves, minced (or 1/2 tsp., 2 mL, powder)	2	2
Can of tomato sauce (7 1/2 oz., 213 mL)	1	1
Brown sugar, packed	1/4 cup	60 mL
Louisiana hot sauce	3 tbsp.	45 mL
Apple cider vinegar	1 tbsp.	15 mL
Dried oregano	2 tsp.	10 mL
Salt	1/2 tsp.	2 mL
Pepper	1/2 tsp.	2 mL

Place ribs in Dutch oven or large pot. Pour beer over top. Add water to
cover. Bring to a boil. Reduce heat to medium-low. Simmer, covered, for
about 1 hour until ribs are tender. Drain.

Melt butter in medium saucepan on medium. Add garlic. Cook for about
5 minutes, stirring often, until fragrant.

Add remaining 7 ingredients. Bring to a boil. Reduce heat to low. Simmer
for 10 minutes to blend flavours. Let stand for about 10 minutes until
slightly cooled. Preheat gas barbecue to medium. Place ribs on greased
grill. Close lid. Cook for about 15 minutes, turning twice and brushing with
tomato mixture until ribs are glazed and heated through. Serves 10.

*1 serving: 378 Calories; 29.2 g Total Fat (12.4 g Mono, 2.1 g Poly, 12.0 g Sat);
110 mg Cholesterol; 7 g Carbohydrate; trace Fibre; 21 g Protein; 465 mg Sodium*

ale-sauced pork roast

Tender pork roast and gravy, deeply flavoured with dark beer and Dijon. The gravy goes well with baked potatoes.

Canola oil	1 tsp.	5 mL
Boneless pork loin roast, trimmed of fat	3 lbs.	1.4 kg
Pepper, sprinkle		
Dark beer	1 1/2 cups	375 mL
Can of condensed onion soup (10 oz., 284 mL)	1	1
Dijon mustard	2 tbsp.	30 mL
Water	1 tbsp.	15 mL
Cornstarch	2 tsp.	10 mL

Heat canola oil in large frying pan on medium-high. Sprinkle roast with pepper. Add to frying pan. Cook for about 8 minutes, turning occasionally, until browned on all sides. Transfer roast to 4 to 5 quart (4 to 5 L) slow cooker. Drain and discard drippings from pan.

Add next 3 ingredients to same frying pan. Heat and stir, scraping any brown bits from bottom of pan, until boiling. Pour over roast. Cook, covered, on Low for 7 to 8 hours or on High for 3 1/2 to 4 hours. Transfer roast to cutting board. Cover with foil. Let stand for 10 minutes. Skim and discard fat from cooking liquid.

Stir water into cornstarch in small cup until smooth. Add to cooking liquid. Stir. Cook, covered, on High for about 10 minutes until boiling and thickened. Thinly slice roast and arrange on large serving plate. Serve with sauce. Serves 8.

1 serving: 291 Calories; 12.5 g Total Fat (5.7 g Mono, 1.3 g Poly, 4.3 g Sat); 96 mg Cholesterol; 5 g Carbohydrate; trace Fibre; 35 g Protein; 427 mg Sodium

irish lentil stew

A warm, rustic stew that's perfect for those cold, blustery days. Serve with bread or biscuits.

Canola oil	2 tsp.	10 mL
Boneless lamb shoulder, trimmed of fat and cut into 1 inch (2.5 cm) pieces	1 1/2 lbs.	680 g
Garlic powder	1/2 tsp.	2 mL
Pepper	1/4 tsp.	1 mL
Chopped onion	2 cups	500 mL
Dark beer	1 cup	250 mL
Low-sodium prepared chicken broth	3 cups	750 mL
Red baby potatoes, larger ones cut in half	1 1/2 lbs.	680 g
Baby carrots	2 cups	500 mL
Chopped celery	1 1/2 cups	375 mL
Dried green lentils	1 cup	250 mL
Dried thyme	1/2 tsp.	2 mL
Bay leaf	1	1
Chopped fresh parsley	2 tbsp.	30 mL

Heat canola oil in Dutch oven on medium-high. Add lamb. Sprinkle with garlic powder and pepper. Cook for about 10 minutes, stirring occasionally, until browned.

Add onion and beer. Heat and stir for 1 minute, scraping any brown bits from bottom of pot.

Add next 7 ingredients. Stir. Bring to a boil. Reduce heat to medium-low. Simmer, covered, for about 2 hours, stirring occasionally, until lamb is tender. Remove and discard bay leaf.

Sprinkle with parsley. Makes about 9 cups (2.25 L).

1 cup (250 mL): 290 Calories; 6 g Total Fat (2 g Mono, 0.5 g Poly, 2 g Sat); 54 mg Cholesterol; 35 g Carbohydrate; 6 g Fibre; 23 g Protein; 276 mg Sodium

stout lamb stew

A rich-flavoured stew with tender lamb balanced by a dark sauce containing stout beer. The combination of ingredients creates a satisfying and complete meal. Serve with biscuits or a baguette.

All-purpose flour	1/4 cup	60 mL
Seasoned salt	1 tsp.	5 mL
Pepper	1/2 tsp.	2 mL
Stewing lamb, trimmed of fat	1 1/2 lbs.	680 g
Chopped peeled potato	2 cups	500 mL
Chopped yellow turnip (rutabaga)	2 cups	500 mL
Sliced fresh white mushrooms	2 cups	500 mL
Sliced onion	1 cup	250 mL
Bay leaves	2	2
Stout beer	1 1/3 cups	325 mL
Prepared beef broth	1 cup	250 mL
Tomato paste (see Tip, page 64)	2 tbsp.	30 mL
Garlic cloves, minced	2	2
(or 1/2 tsp., 2 mL, powder)		
Balsamic vinegar	1 tbsp.	15 mL

Combine first 3 ingredients in large resealable freezer bag. Add lamb. Seal bag. Toss until coated. Transfer lamb to greased 4 quart (4 L) casserole. Reserve remaining flour mixture.

Scatter next 5 ingredients over lamb.

Whisk next 4 ingredients and reserved flour mixture in medium bowl. Pour over vegetables. Stir. Cook, covered, in 350°F (175°C) oven for about 2 hours until lamb and vegetables are tender. Remove and discard bay leaves.

Add vinegar. Stir. Makes about 8 cups (2 L).

1 cup (250 mL): 342 Calories; 23.0 g Total Fat (7.0 g Mono, 1.0 g Poly, 11.0 g Sat); 68 mg Cholesterol; 17 g Carbohydrate; 2 g Fibre; 17 g Protein; 334 mg Sodium

moroccan lamb shanks

Serve with couscous and a side of carrots, and garnish with fresh chopped mint.

Apricot beer	2/3 cup	150 mL
Medium onions, cut into	2	2
1/4 inch (6 mm) slices		
Cinnamon sticks	2	2
Salt	1/2 tsp.	2 mL
Apricot jam	2 tbsp.	30 mL
Garlic cloves, minced	6	6
Ground cumin	1 tbsp.	15 mL
Ketchup	1 tbsp.	15 mL
Ground cinnamon	2 tsp.	10 mL
Salt	1 tsp.	5 mL
Pepper	1/2 tsp.	2 mL
Lamb shanks	6	6
(about 3/4 lb., 340 g, each)		

Combine first 4 ingredients in greased 9 x 13 inch (23 x 33 cm) foil pan.

Combine next 7 ingredients and spread over lamb shanks. Sear on direct medium-high heat for about 8 minutes, turning every 2 to 3 minutes, until browned. Arrange lamb over onion mixture and cover tightly with foil. Cook on direct medium-high heat for 10 minutes, then turn off burner under pan, leaving opposite burner on. Cook for about 3 hours, rotating pan 180° every hour, until lamb is fork-tender. Transfer lamb to serving plate and cover to keep warm. Remove and discard cinnamon sticks. Skim and discard fat from pan. In blender or food processor, carefully process onion mixture until smooth, following manufacturer's instructions for processing hot liquids. Serve with lamb. Serves 6.

1 serving: 521 Calories; 25.4 g Total Fat (10.7 g Mono, 1.8 g Poly, 10.3 g Sat); 181 mg Cholesterol; 11 g Carbohydrate; 1 g Fibre; 54 g Protein; 753 mg Sodium

chipotle cream sauce

Spicy, smoky, rich and creamy, this sauce works well with any pasta. For best results, use a lager.

Cooking oil	1 tsp.	5 mL
Chopped onion	1 cup	250 mL
Finely chopped chipotle peppers in adobo sauce (see Tip, page 64)	1 tbsp.	15 mL
Garlic cloves, minced (or 1/2 tsp., 2 mL, powder)	2	2
Granulated sugar	1 tsp.	5 mL
Ground cumin	1 tsp.	5 mL
Ground ginger	1 tsp.	5 mL
Salt	1/2 tsp.	5 mL
Pepper	1/4 tsp.	1 mL
All-purpose flour	1 tbsp.	15 mL
Can of diced tomatoes (28 oz., 796 mL), with juice	1	1
Chopped roasted red pepper	1/2 cup	125 mL
Beer	1/3 cup	75 mL
Whipping cream	1 cup	250 mL

Heat cooking oil in medium saucepan on medium. Add next 8 ingredients. Cook, uncovered, for 5 to 10 minutes, stirring often, until onion is softened.

Add flour. Heat and stir for 1 minute.

Add next 3 ingredients. Heat and stir until boiling and thickened. Carefully process with hand blender or in blender until smooth, following manufacturer's instructions for processing hot liquids.

Add cream. Stir. Store in airtight container in refrigerator for up to 3 days or in freezer for up to 1 month. Makes about 5 1/2 cups (1/4 L).

1 cup (250 mL): 132 Calories; 4 g Total Fat (0.5 g Mono, 0.3 g Poly, 2.3 g Sat); 15 mg Cholesterol; 20 g Carbohydrate; 1 g Fibre; 3 g Protein; 826 mg Sodium

dark bean chili

Black beans, mushrooms and onions sautéed until well-browned make this dish darker than most chili recipes.

Cooking oil	2 tbsp.	30 mL
Fresh brown (or white) mushrooms quartered	2 lbs.	900 g
Chopped onion	1 1/2 cups	375 mL
Beer	1 cup	250 mL
Cans of black beans (19 oz., 540 mL, each) rinsed and drained	2	2
Can of crushed tomatoes (28 oz., 796 mL)	1	1
Can of red kidney beans (14 oz., 398 mL) rinsed and drained	1	1
Water	1 1/2 cups	375 mL
Tomato paste (see Tip, page 64)	1/4 cup	60 mL
Dried oregano	1 1/2 tsp.	7 mL
Ground cumin	1 1/2 tsp.	7 mL
Granulated sugar	1 tsp.	5 mL
Salt	3/4 tsp.	4 mL
Ground chipotle pepper	1/2 tsp.	2 mL
Chopped fresh cilantro (or parsley)	1/3 cup	75 mL
Steak sauce	1/4 cup	60 mL

Heat cooking oil in Dutch oven on medium-high. Add mushrooms and onion. Cook for about 15 minutes, stirring often, until mushrooms are browned and onion is softened. Reduce heat to medium. Add beer. Simmer for 5 minutes. Transfer to 3 1/2 to 4 quart (3.5 to 4 L) slow cooker.

Add next 10 ingredients. Stir. Cook, covered, on Low for 8 to 9 hours or on High for 4 to 4 1/2 hours.

Stir in cilantro and steak sauce. Makes about 11 cups (2.75 L).

1 cup (250 mL): 160 Calories; 3 g Total Fat (1.5 g Mono, 0.5 g Poly, 0 g Sat); 0 mg Cholesterol; 23 g Carbohydrate; 7 g Fibre; 8 g Protein; 510 mg Sodium

recipe index

topical tips

Chipotle peppers: Chipotle chili peppers in adobo sauce are smoked jalapeño peppers that are canned in a smoky red sauce. Adobo sauce is not as spicy as the chipotle pepper, but it still packs some heat. Be sure to wash your hands after handling. Store leftover chipotle chili peppers with sauce in airtight container in refrigerator for up to 1 year.

Chopping hot peppers: Hot peppers contain capsaicin in the seeds and ribs. Removing the seeds and ribs will reduce the heat. Wear rubber gloves when handling hot peppers and avoid touching your eyes. Wash your hands well afterwards.

Tomato paste: If a recipe calls for less than an entire can of tomato paste, freeze the unopened can for 30 minutes. Open both ends and push the contents through one end. Slice off only what you need. Freeze the remaining paste in a resealable freezer bag or plastic wrap for future use.

Nutrition Information Guidelines

Each recipe is analyzed using the Canadian Nutrient File from Health Canada, which is based on the United States Department of Agriculture (USDA) Nutrient Database.

- If more than one ingredient is listed (such as "butter or hard margarine"), or if a range is given (1 – 2 tsp., 5 – 10 mL), only the first ingredient or first amount is analyzed.

- For meat, poultry and fish, the serving size per person is based on the recommended 4 oz. (113 g) uncooked weight (without bone), which is 2 – 3 oz. (57 – 85 g) cooked weight (without bone) — approximately the size of a deck of playing cards.

- Milk used is 1% M.F. (milk fat), unless otherwise stated.

- Cooking oil used is canola oil, unless otherwise stated.

- Ingredients indicating "sprinkle," "optional" or "for garnish" are not included in the nutrition information.

- The fat in recipes and combination foods can vary greatly depending on the sources and types of fats used in each specific ingredient. For these reasons, the count of saturated, monounsaturated and polyunsaturated fats may not add up to the total fat content.